ECHOES OF A LANDSCAPE ○ SHAI GINOTT

ECHOES OF A LANDSCAPE

PHOTOGRAPHED BY SHAI GINOTT

MOD Publishing House

Graphic design: Nomi Morag

English translation: Aloma Halter

ISBN 965-05-0655-1

Production manager: Shalom Zadok
Typesetting: Art Plus, Jerusalem
Color separation: Scanli Ltd. Tel Aviv
Plates and Printing: Grapholite Print, Tel Aviv

All photos were taken with Olympus cameras: OM-4, OM-4Ti; on Fujichrome films
Film development: Jeffrey Cohen Laboratory, Tel Aviv; Ronnie Heymann, Jerusalem

To my parents, Irit and Noah,
my sister Shimrit and brother Yari

To...

Esther Tishby for the knowledge and enthusiasm she brought to helping me choose the poetry texts; to Carmela Abder whose comments on the manuscript and on the choice of photos were extremely stimulating; to Nomi Morag for the painstaking and sensitive design of the book; to Mordechai Shalev, Sabina and Professor Schweid, to Ronnie Heymann and Yael Gouri and to Miri Siegler-Eliya for their professional help and invaluable advice; to my friends and all those close to me, for their support and encouragement to publish these photographs — my heartfelt thanks.

Shai Ginott

It is to the place that I love
That my feet lead me.

Hillel the Elder,
Babylonian Talmud: *Sukkah* 53

INTRODUCTION

I stood on the cliff north of Netanya, beneath me viscous swirls of lava along the edge of a golden strip. A barefoot man, holding his sandals, strolled past... □   What is it that transforms a commonplace occurance — a man walking by the seashore on a bright, sunlit day — to this live drama? Not the water, not even the sand or the light; but the moment of encounter between them all, and between them and myself. I seek out such meetings: the interlacing relationships between light, earth, water, the sky, and man. To see, to capture in a photograph the way they find mutual expression. Through my lens I seek to expand a field of vision and be renewed within it. When the camera shutter dilates, I also take in the picture; inside me both aesthetic and sensual pleasures from the contact with Nature intertwine. □   Four chapters complement one another in this book: light, earth, water and sky. In each chapter, one of them assumes "centre stage", while the others accompany it, playing supporting roles. □   All the pictures were taken in Israel between 1988-1991. □   Sometimes, when we are transfixed by Nature, exposed to its colours and scents, touching its smooth and its grainy textures with equal sensitivity, attentive to the silence and the rustlings, the flow of water and of wind, following the shifting light throughout the four seasons of the year — a sensation is formed within us, an echo of the exterior landscape. I call this special moment the fifth season: a season without time limits, a private affair. □   For me, photographing Nature means to be involved without interferring, gazing at the object, not "staging" it. I return to the particular shell, the cloud, the ripples. I discover a landscape in the detail of a leaf, in the stamen of a poppy. Each time, I'm astonished afresh. I stalk the moment until it appears in all its intensity; nothing is taken for granted. And above all, there's the magic. I was enchanted by the possibilities of photographing landscapes here in Israel, sights which to all intents and purposes might have been shot anywhere in the world; of crossing the boundries of tangible reality, equipped only with a camera, going beyond the borders of Israel — all the way to the utmost limits of the universe. Like standing on the edge of the cliff at Netanya and seeing the currents of lava. □   Nature photography is like poetry, a reflection of personal experience. That's why I was drawn to "illustrate" the pictures with reflective passages and poems.

LIGHT

In the midst of youth, on life's sea was I cast

And all my life longed for seclusion, tranquility;

I panted for light from the world's body vast,

while something I knew not, like wine surged in me.

I explored secret places. There my gaze was rivetted

in the eye of the world — an observer was my part;

there my friends were revealed me, their secrets received

and I sealed their voices close in my mute heart.

Hayim Nahman Bialik

He wraps himself in light as if it were a garment

He spreads out the sky as if it were a curtain.

Psalms 104:2

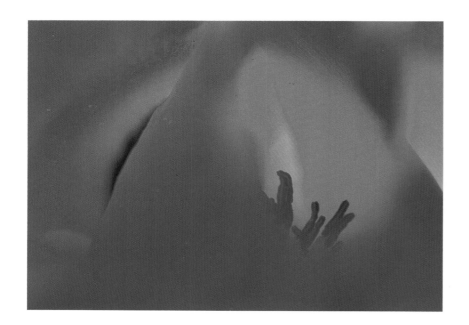

And deepen my senses, broaden them
to steep in a verdant world, bud and green shoot
absorbing from them the secret
of the budding in my stillness.

Hillel Bavli

And so I said to Autumn, which rose from the cascade of leaf-fall

Greetings, dear friend, glimpsed from the cloud rends,

I didn't know your landscape could be travesed like this at all,

Or that I would see your features so resemble my own.

Haim Gouri

The light,

light of our city,

what does it do,

what does it do by itself, by itself,

when we close our eyes for a moment?

When it remains by itself

alone and rumbling,

the light of giants,

light without anyone to see it,

from that beyond to the red screen

of my eyelids pressed tight together.

Natan Alterman

And the wandering light like a prince in love

and the chill of silver and the heat of gold.

Dalia Ravikovitch

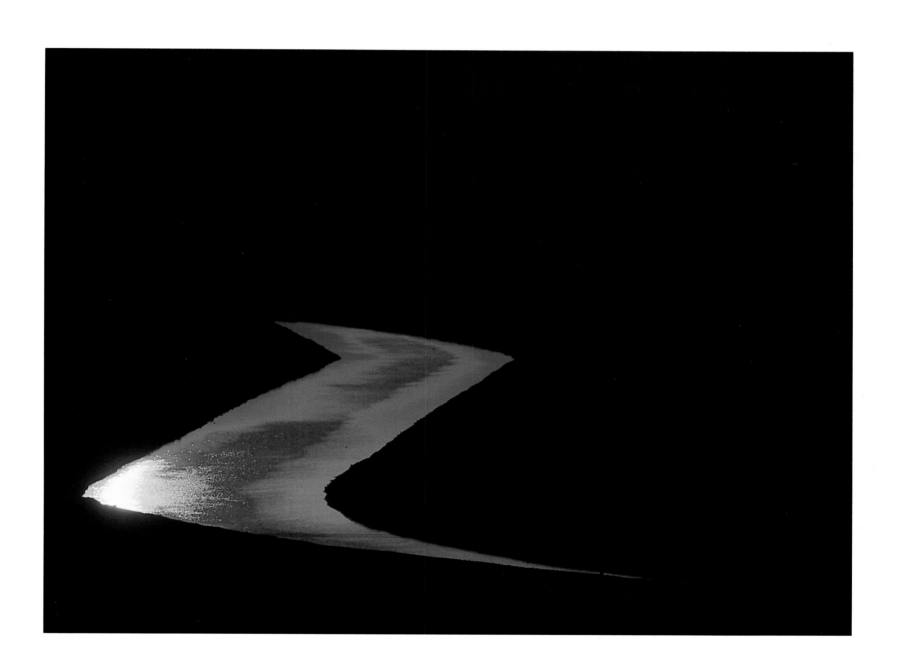

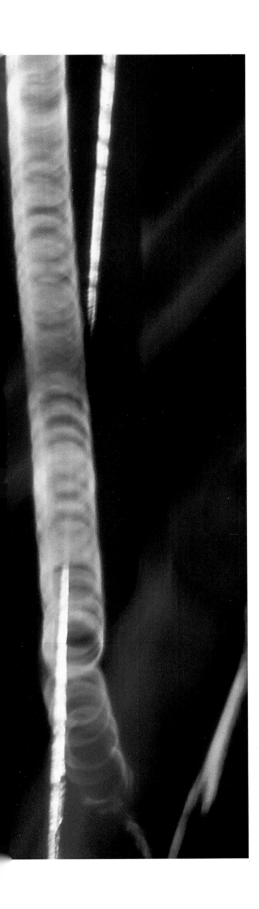

It's not the hand, far more the eyes

whoever can see it — will be able to draw,

and if not draw — to sing

the translucency of the air, the draining of colour by the sun

borrowing the hues of the trees — to the sun, the stubble to the sun,

the way of the summer with the sun, and it's translucency

Mira Meir

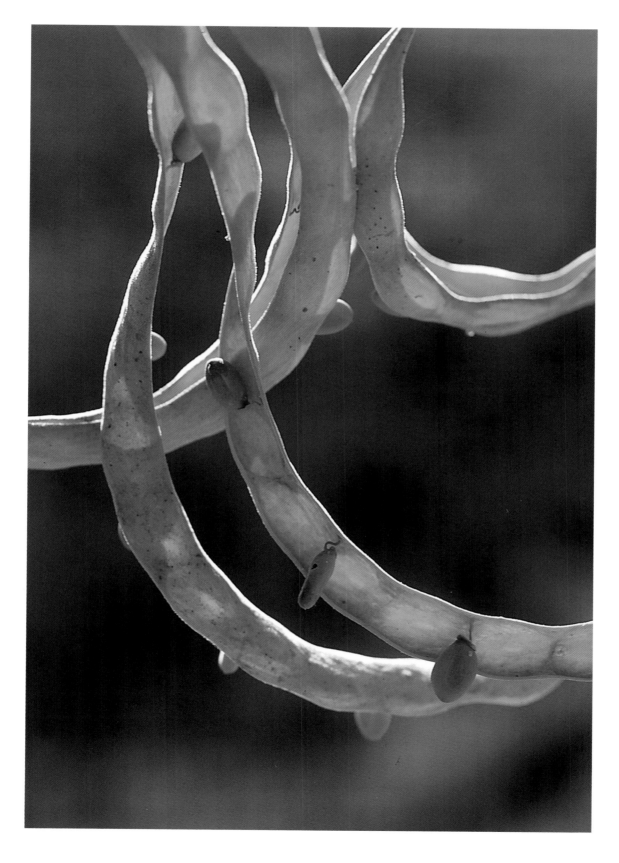

The sun rises

and the sun goes down

and hastens to the place

of its rising

Ecclesiastes 1:5

If man

were to pull a thread behind him

to every place he goes,

what trace would be left behind him,

what pattern,

from one place to the next, a fine line

on the face of the earth.

a sensitive and precise sketch

which is always vibrant.

Haya Shenhav

...And from the song of the grass

is the shepherd's tune made.

Rabbi Nahman of Bratslav

EARTH

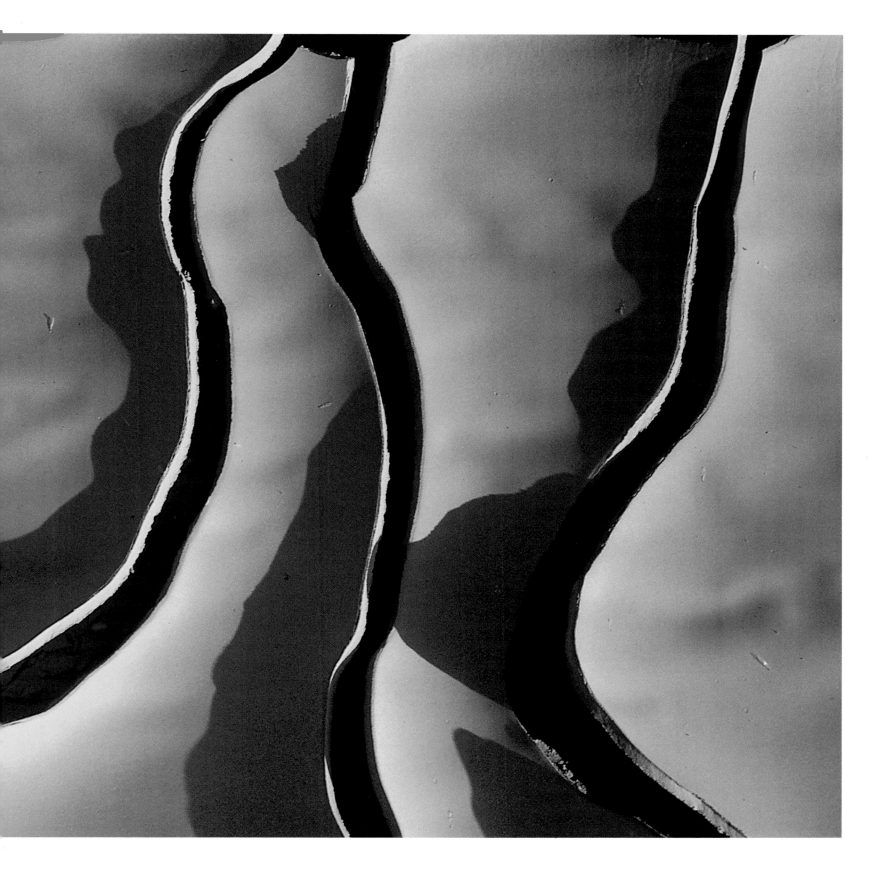

That which I didn't read in prayer and hymn books

I read in the hills.

In the hills I proclaim

all the supplications and psalms.

From the deep valley I learnt

the heart's cry, as if from a prison.

And pure prayers

I learnt from the azure skies.

On the hilltops I saw engraved

all exaltation.

And all the verses inscribed

on the bare and stricken slopes.

And all words of wrath

within the cliffs.

Yitzhak Shalev

The Holy One, Blessed be He,

set aside the names

of animate and inanimate objects

and did not reveal them to Adam,

in order that he might name them

by observing them

and so come to know their essence and nature

and the names appropriate to them.

Sefer Ha'Aggadah

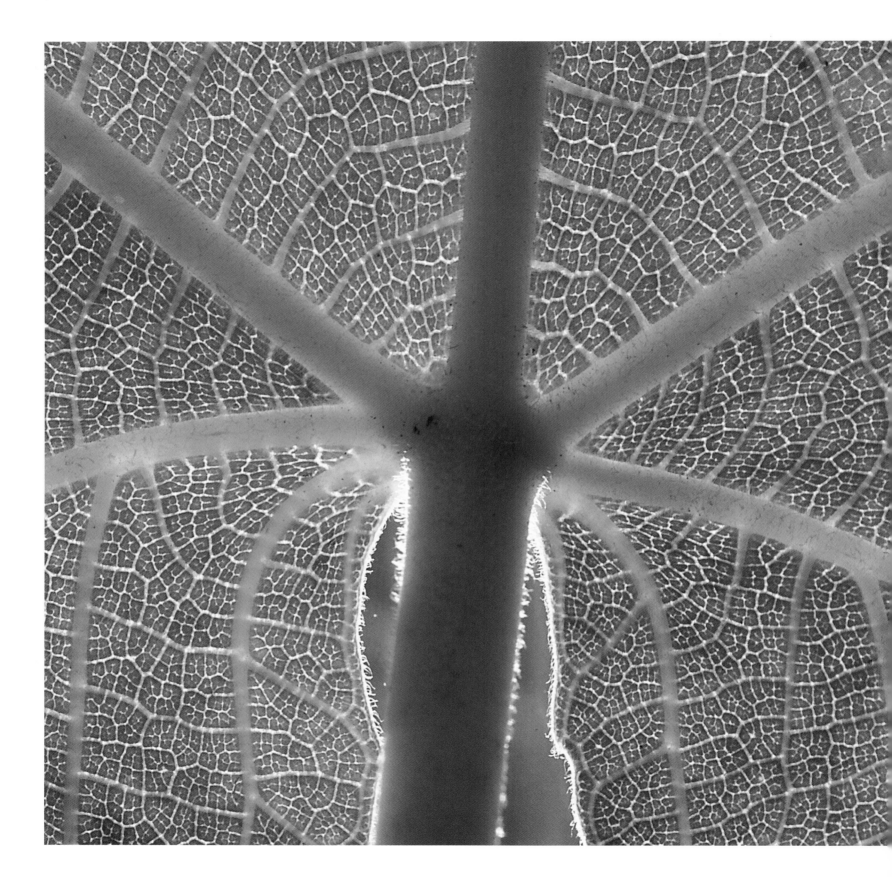

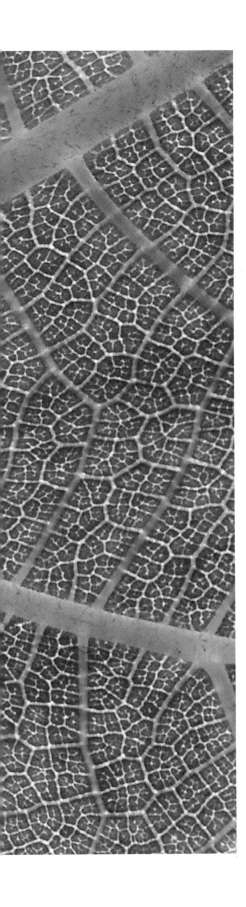

And perhaps in a far distant incarnation

I was a greenish blade of grass?

Thus I cling to mother earth,

and in her swarthy bosom find repose.

Rachel

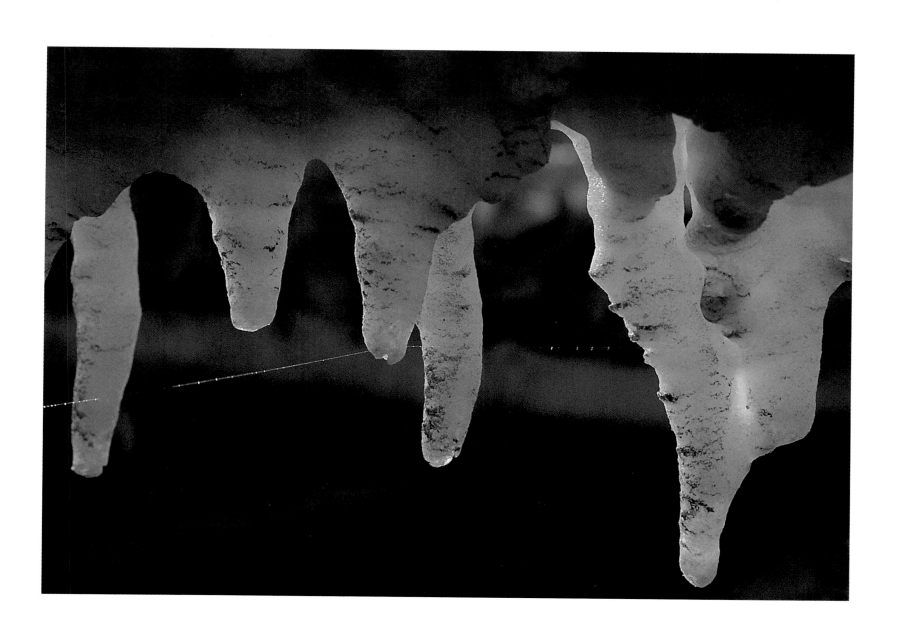

Roads have no eyes with which to see

the intensity of the dreams

of those who travel them.

Avraham Chalfi

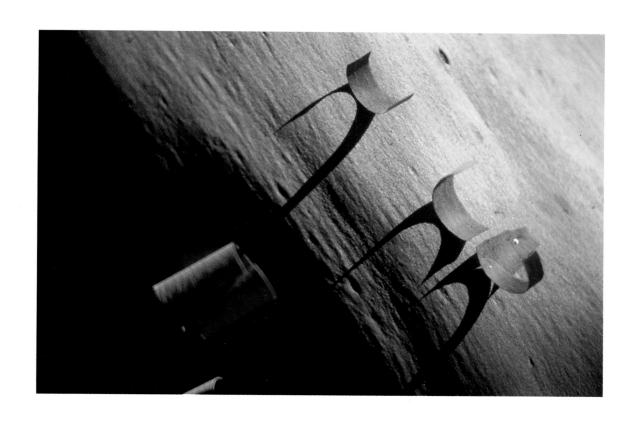

And the earth — a giant piano

its keys — a thousand thousand

its tunes — ten thousand thousand

but when I play it with my bare feet

and its tunes get together:

it's me!

Avraham Shlonsky

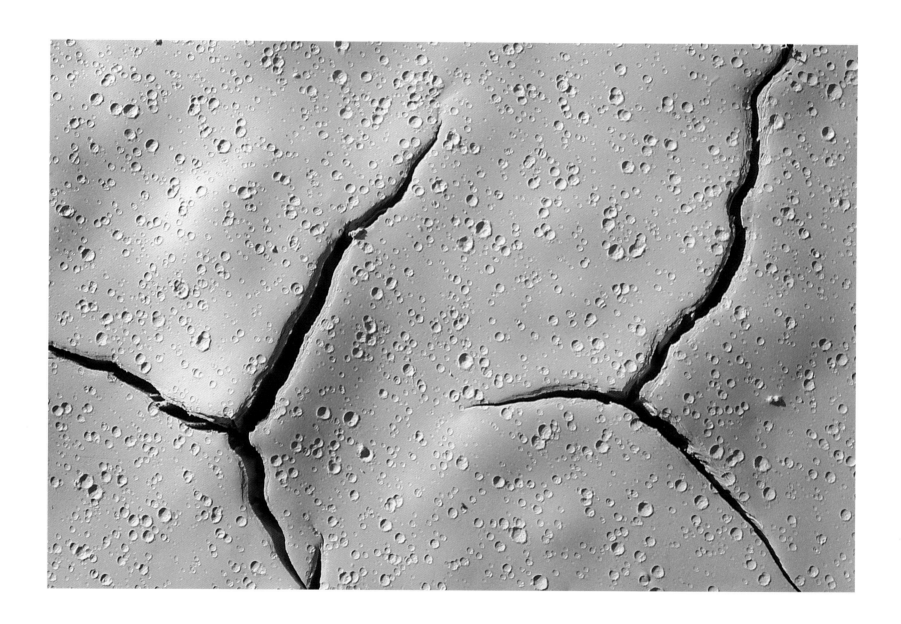

And we follow the contour of the hill

that leads towards the light

that returns and leads the things

we are gazing at,

helping them to come into being.

Israel Eliraz

Here are the trees with their chattering leaves.

Here the air, intoxicated by its height.

I don't want

to write them.

I want to touch their hearts.

Natan Alterman

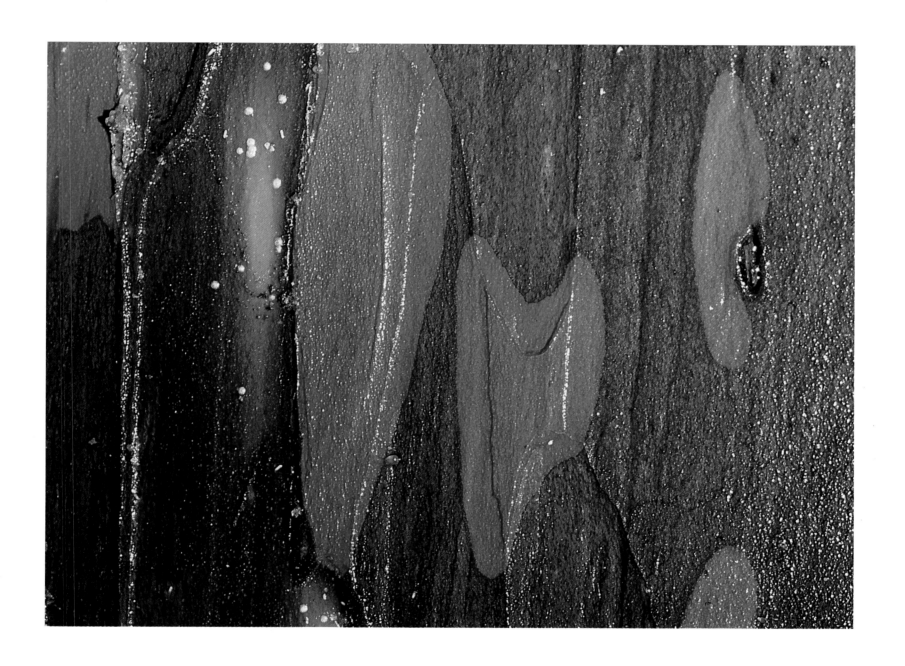

For man, since he is a man, always needs to live within nature,

since to man nature is the very sensation and tangibility that water is to fish.

Man needs not only the reflection of nature's image in his soul,

but requires the sphere of nature's influence

for a unifying, all-encompassing pressure.

For it is nature itself whose eternal existence weighs upon each

of the points of contact of man's body and his soul,

compelling him to be, to exist as a man and to become an individual.

A.D. Gordon

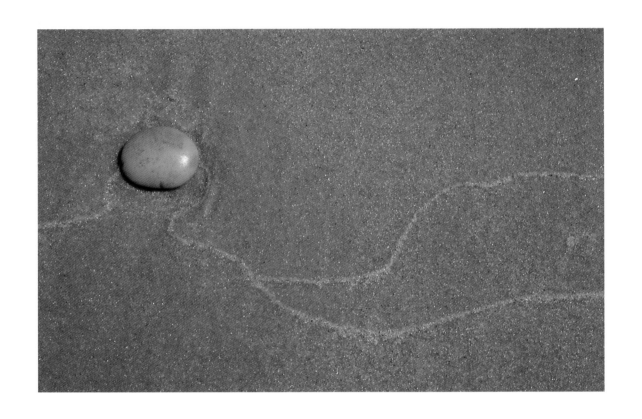

And all of a sudden

from the heights of the azure

a wilderness filled with cast stones

was revealed.

Leah Goldberg

The azure of the prayer shawl resembles the sea

and the sea resembles the grass

and the grass resembles the heavens.

Jerusalem Talmud, *Berakhot* 1:2

All things in the Heavens above and on the Earth beneath, all were bestowed from a lofty place,

and for this reason the Righteous would be careful not to speak ill of any of God's creatures.

Moshe Cordovero

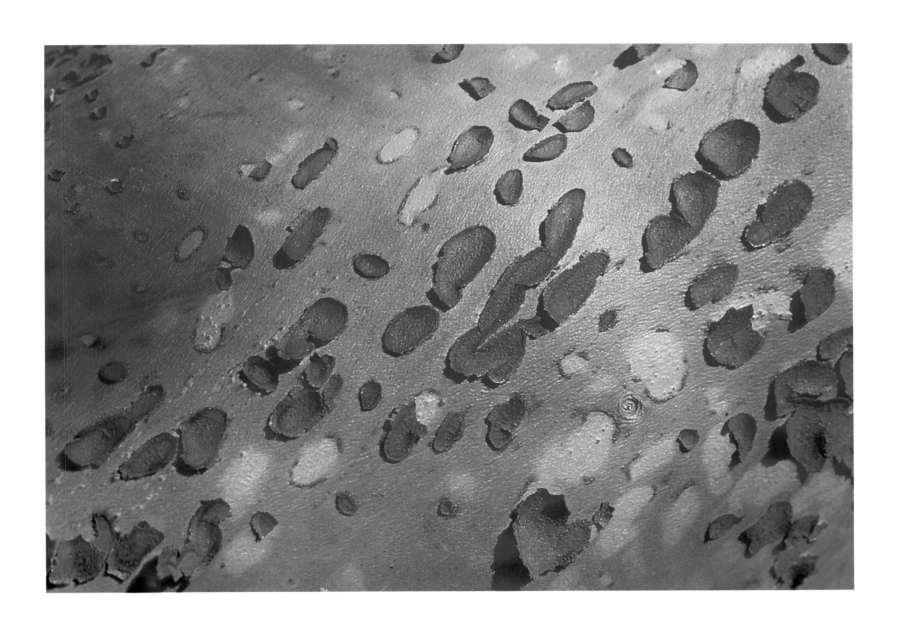

The entire day the mountain gazed
at your little hand, plucking wild flowers.
The entire day the mountain inclined its huge ear
to your song, attentive.

And in the evening it accompanied your return
with long shadows.
And then the thought suffused your heart
that the mountain loved you.

Judith Kafri

WATER

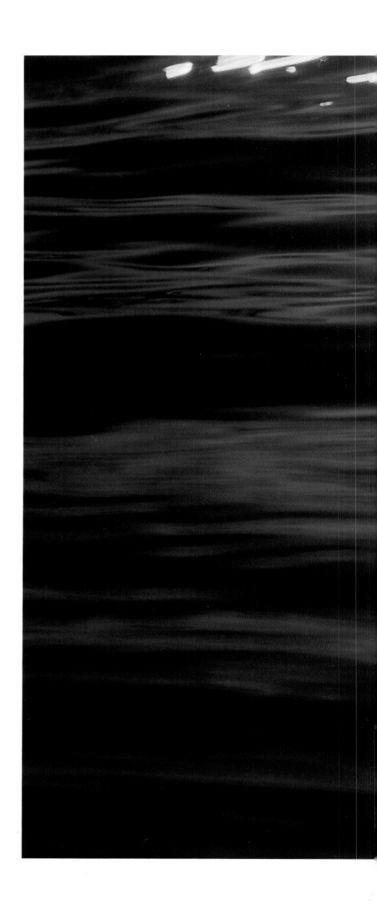

Since

the wind hasn't

anyone to write letters to her

its froth issues forth white

and she plays like crazy over the waves

but in the season of migration

birds write her across the skies,

gloomy musical scores

and the shadow of a passing cloud.

Gad Aviassaf

The waves raged   like the spinning of wheels

both thunderous and giddy   upon the surface of the sea,

the sky grew sombre   and its waters seethed

while the depths were heaved up   and bore surging waves.

Rabbi Yehuda Halevi

Sometimes the rain falls on account

of the merits of a single person,

or a single blade of grass.

Jerusalem Talmud, *Ta'anit* 3:2

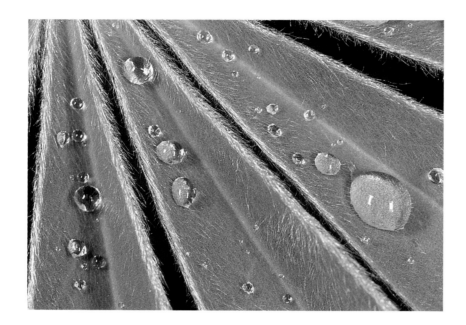

The wind stirred branches
And shook the raindrops from them
And as the raindrops were sprayed
they caught the light in their net.

Natan Alterman

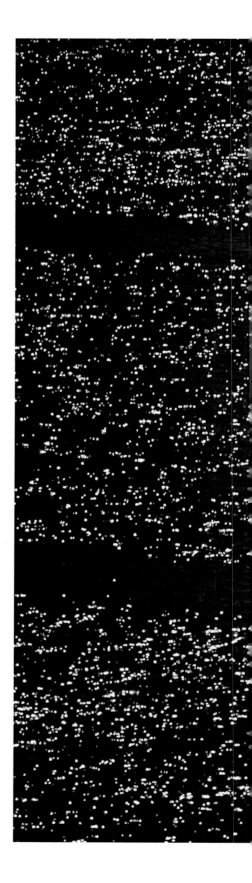

Three things preceded the creation of the world:

Water, wind and fire.

The water conceived and bore darkness,

The fire conceived and bore light,

The wind conceived and bore wisdom.

It is with these six that the world is conducted:

With wind and wisdom,

with fire and light,

with darkness and water.

Sefer Ha'Aggadah

He made sand as the border of the sea / As a man makes a fence around his vineyard /

And when the water floods over its banks / And sees the sand before it / It immediately retreats /

Sefer Ha'Aggadah

I bring everything I find.

Not everything that glitters is gold.

But I pick up

everything that glitters.

Avot Yeshurun

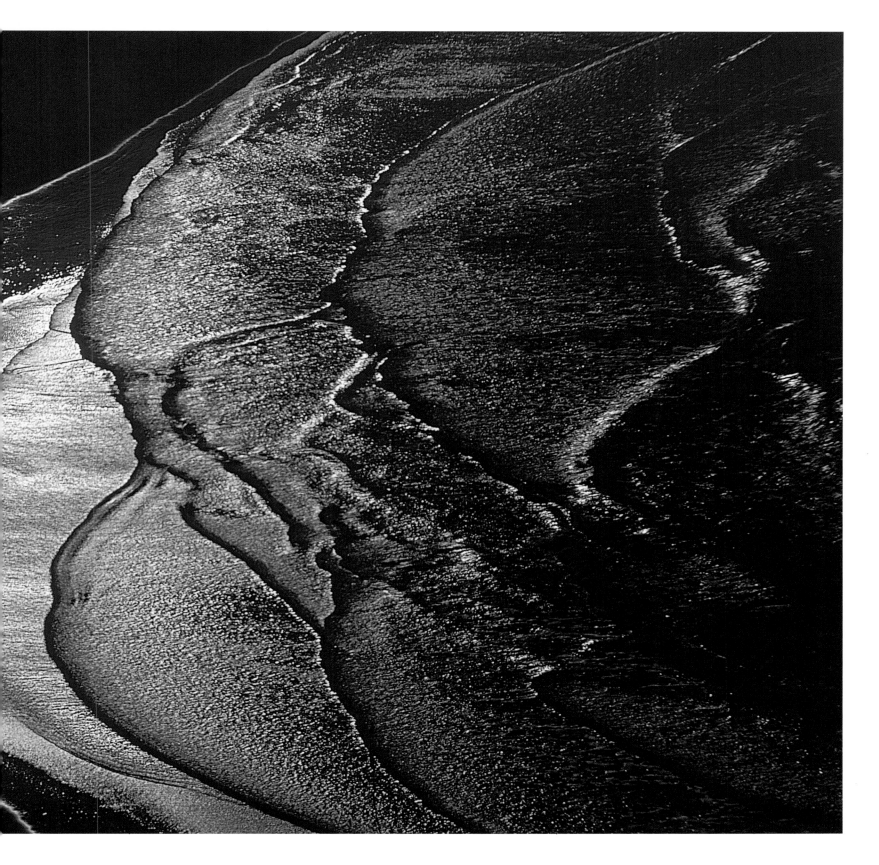

SKY

And with soft ropes to draw up my heart
skyward. To become a white cloud
drunk with light.

A white cloud
which a soft breeze stirs gently
forever.

Rachel Negev

And the birches, tall, still beating

leaves dry as bones, and the scant gold

still intertwined in them

embroidered like a thought

about nothing

Dan Armon

Shaul sits stooped in the cloud of his heaviness.

His forehead, drooping is cast in the darkness of his hand.

In the distance above, like a moon circling,

David drifts on the melody.

Tuvia Rübner

In the beginning God created

the heavens that really are not

and the earth that wants to touch them.

In the beginning God created

cords stretched between them

between the heavens that really are not

and the earth crying out.

And the man he created

the man who is prayer and cord

who touches that which is not

with a touch light and soft.

Rivka Miriam

...for the skies have been filled by wind

which all the skies will not imprison.

Shmuel Shatal

There are six and thirty unseen birds

whose virtue upholds the sky.

Avraham Shlonsky

With the kindling of summer in the skies,

a hush will flow like a distant echo of water.

Avraham Chalfi

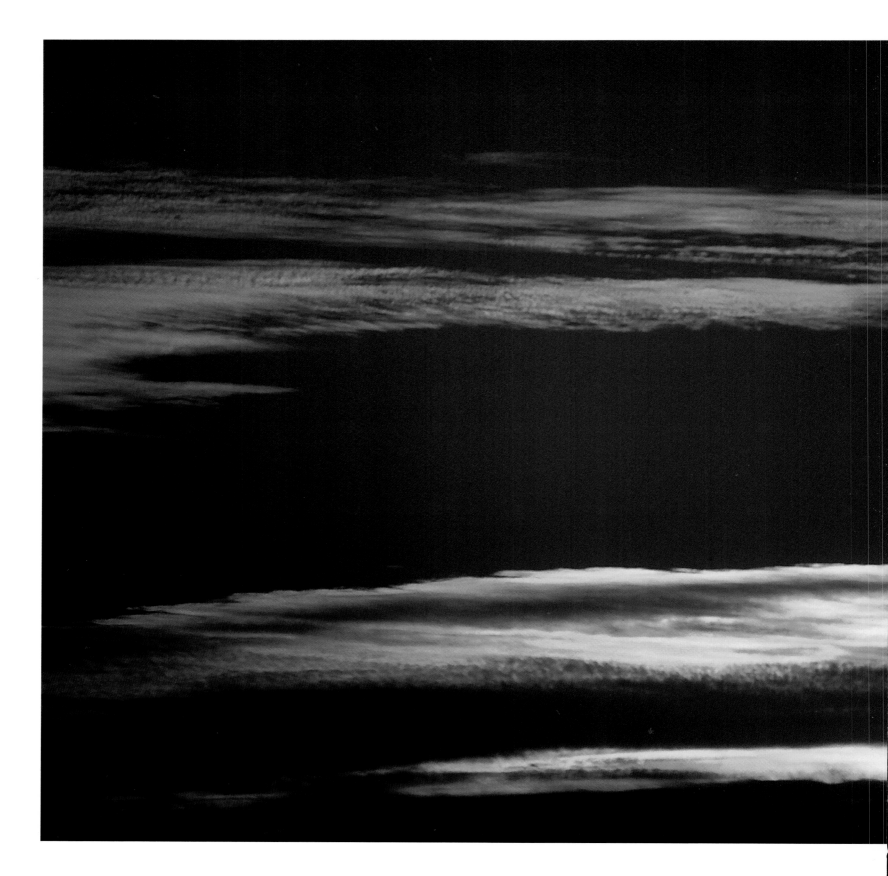

The entire Fall the clouds wept, until at last

the trees languishing in the fields revived.

Shlomo Ibn Gavirol

By night Jerusalem grows taller

As if someone lifts her onto the crown of his head

And walks with her deep among the stars.

Israel Ephrat

SOURCES OF THE HEBREW TEXTS

The texts were translated by:

Aloma Halter: Jacket, preface, preliminary, end pages; 18, 21, 22, 28, 39, 46, 54, 59, 62, 67, 72, 79, 80, 84, 97, 102, 122, 124, 127, 132, 134, 136, 141

Aloma Halter with Shmuel Himelsteim: 12, 98

Shmuel Himelsteim: 7, 16, 34, 41, 50, 83, 100, 110, 139

Harold Schimmel: 114 (courtesy Institute for the Translation of Hebrew Literature)

Linda Zisquit: 129

Translation by the poets: 31, 86

THE PICTURES